METALS
AND ALLOYS

© Aladdin Books Ltd 1987

Designed and produced by
Aladdin Books Ltd
70 Old Compton Street
London W1

First published in the
United States in 1988 by
Gloucester Press
387 Park Avenue South
New York, NY 10016

ISBN 0-531-17083-7

Library of Congress Catalog
Card Number: 87-82902

Printed in Belgium

Design	David West Children's Book Design
Editor	Margaret Fagan
Researcher	Cecilia Weston-Baker
Illustrators	Louise Nevett Simon Bishop
Consultant	Ian Mercer Geological Museum, London

CONTENTS

Photographic Credits:
Cover and pages 13 and 25: Tony Stone Associates; title page: Topham Picture Library; page 4-5: Art Directors; pages 6, 9 (top) and 16: Robert Harding; pages 8 and 21: Anglo-American Corporation; page 9 (bottom) and 10: Hutchison Library; pages 15 and 23: Paul Brierley; page 18: Vanessa Bailey; page 19: Leo Mason; page 20: Spectrum.

RESOURCES TODAY

METALS
AND ALLOYS

Kathryn Whyman

GLOUCESTER PRESS
New York · London · Toronto · Sydney

WHAT IS A METAL?

Metals play a very important part in our lives. Cars, trains and airplanes are all made of metals. We use metals for building houses and bridges. Our electricity is carried along metal cables, and industries use metal machinery. Look around and you will notice how different metals are used for different jobs. Copper can be drawn into thin wires and used in electricity cables. Aluminum can be rolled into thin sheets and is ideal for metal foil.

Many metals are good conductors of electricity

The world is made up of thousands of different substances – water, salt and wood are just a few examples. But all of these substances are made up from one or more of about 100 basic substances called elements, and 70 of these elements are metals. Though all the metals are different they do have some things in common. They are all shiny. Heat and electricity can travel along all metals. Metals can be mixed together to make substances called alloys. Brass is an alloy.

HOW ARE METALS FORMED?

Metals are found as minerals in the ground. Only a few are ever found as pure metals – copper, gold, silver and platinum can all be found in this way. Metals are usually combined with other elements. Iron and aluminum usually combine with oxygen, for example. Most of the minerals we use are scattered thinly through the rocks. But sometimes they are found in large quantities in one place and are worth extracting. When minerals are concentrated like this they are called ores. Geologists, who understand how rocks form and where ores are likely to be, suggest areas to be explored and drilled. If the test is successful, the area may be mined.

Rock is drilled from the ground to test for gold

The diagram shows how metals can become concentrated in the earth's crust. In some places there are pools of molten rock – magma – within the crust. As magma cools, rocks form. Any liquid left is a mixture of very hot water and minerals. This mixture may (1) react with nearby rocks and deposit minerals. The hot water may (2) seep into cracks in the rock layers, (3) react with rocks such as limestone or (4) seep through volcanic lava. Rainwater (5) may seep into the rocks, pick up minerals and deposit them in cracks. Ancient sea water trapped in rock layers may warm up and deposit minerals in cracks (6) or seep through the sea bed as springs (7). Flowing water (8) may carry minerals and deposit them on the sea bed. The inset shows how a typical deposit of minerals may look with the surrounding rocks removed.

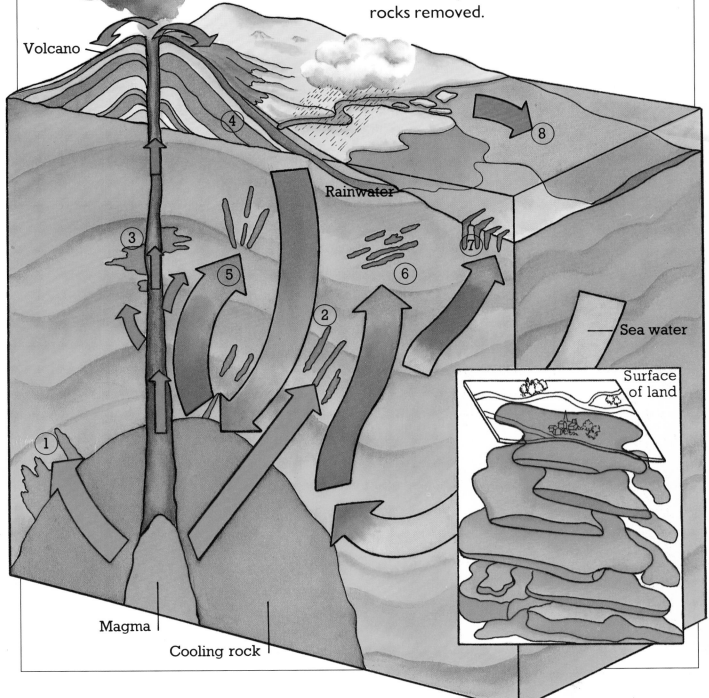

Volcano

Rainwater

Sea water

Surface of land

Magma

Cooling rock

MINING FOR METAL

Once the metals have been found the next job is to find out how much is there and if it is worth mining. Fortunately, many large ore deposits are near the surface. Mining at the surface is called open pit mining. The miners use huge machines called excavators to remove any soil or rock covering the deposit. If the deposit is hard it may need to be blasted with explosives to break it up before it is collected.

Mining underground is much more dangerous. A deep shaft is dug and several tunnels are dug out from it. The ore usually is blasted free.

Where metals lie deposited in rocks in water they can be collected by dredging. Then, the metals are separated from the other rock.

Some gold mines in South Africa are over 3,800 meters (4,155 yards) deep

Dredging for tin in Malaysia

Open pit copper mining – excavators carry the deposit and soil to waiting railroad cars

IRON

Of all the metals, iron is the most important to us. This is mainly because it can be made into the alloy steel. Iron is one of the most widely available metals – more iron is produced each year than all the other metals put together.

Most iron ore is a chemical mixture of iron with oxygen and silicon. Before it can be used the iron metal must be separated from the oxygen and silicon in a process called smelting. Smelting is usually carried out in a blast furnace. The hot liquid metal made in the blast furnace is usually ladled away as melt. Some of this melt is poured into sand molds to make cast iron objects. Cast iron is important for use in the car industry.

Iron can also be smelted in an electric furnace

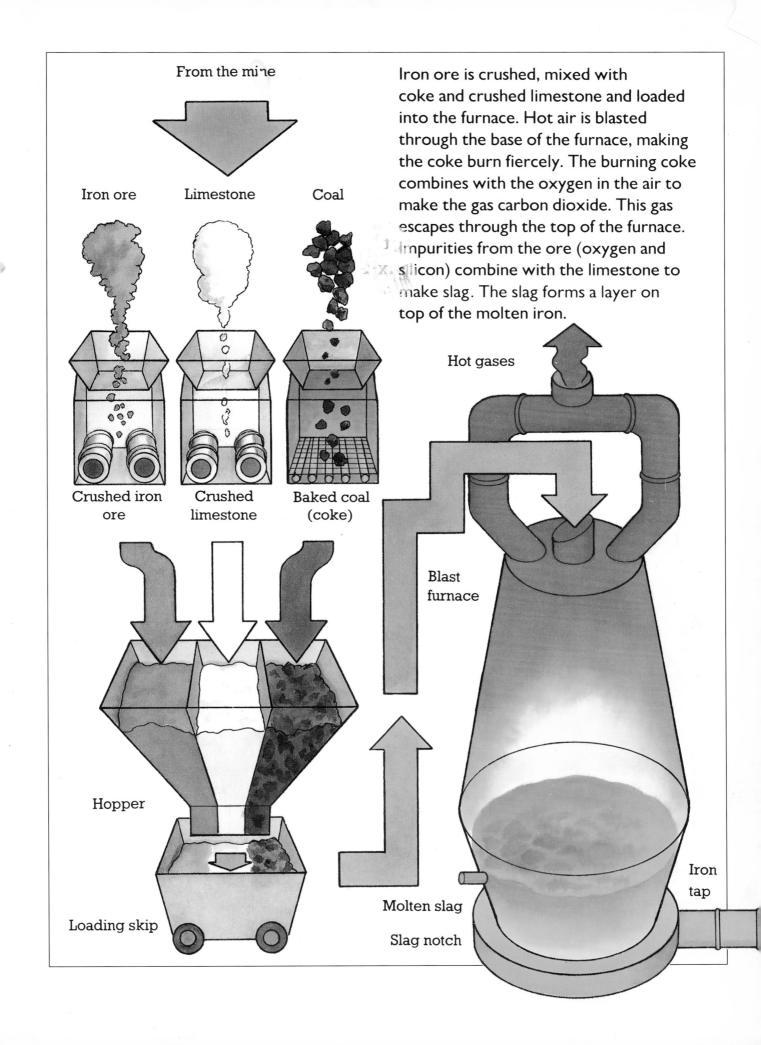

From the mine

Iron ore   Limestone   Coal

Iron ore is crushed, mixed with coke and crushed limestone and loaded into the furnace. Hot air is blasted through the base of the furnace, making the coke burn fiercely. The burning coke combines with the oxygen in the air to make the gas carbon dioxide. This gas escapes through the top of the furnace. Impurities from the ore (oxygen and silicon) combine with the limestone to make slag. The slag forms a layer on top of the molten iron.

Crushed iron ore   Crushed limestone   Baked coal (coke)

Hot gases

Blast furnace

Hopper

Loading skip

Molten slag

Slag notch

Iron tap

MAKING STEEL

Iron is a brittle metal and can easily crack. This is because it contains a lot of carbon from the coke used in the blast furnace. But iron can be used to make steel.

Steel is a mixture. Like iron, it contains carbon. But unlike iron, the amount of carbon is very small. Instead of weakening the metal, this small amount of carbon actually strengthens it. Steel is the most important metal in the building industry because it is extremely strong and it is fairly cheap to produce. Steel and iron are both magnetic.

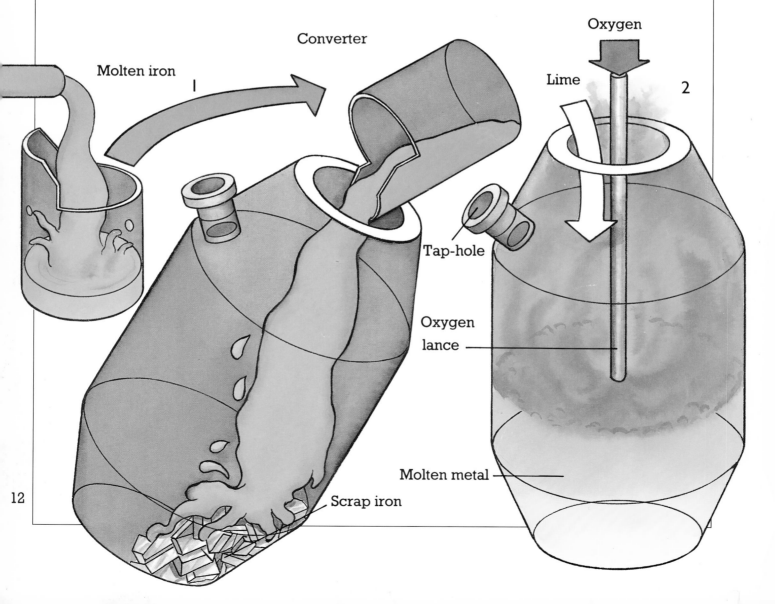

Molten iron

Converter

1

Oxygen

Lime

2

Tap-hole

Oxygen lance

Molten metal

Scrap iron

Molten iron and scrap iron are poured into a huge conical vessel called a converter (1). A jet of pure oxygen is then blasted on to the liquid metal at great speed from a tube (2). The oxygen gets into the metal and burns the carbon until the right amount is left to make steel. Lime combines with impurities in the iron to make slag. This floats on top of the newly made steel. The converter is tipped and the steel and slag are poured into separate ladles (3) and (4).

Making steel

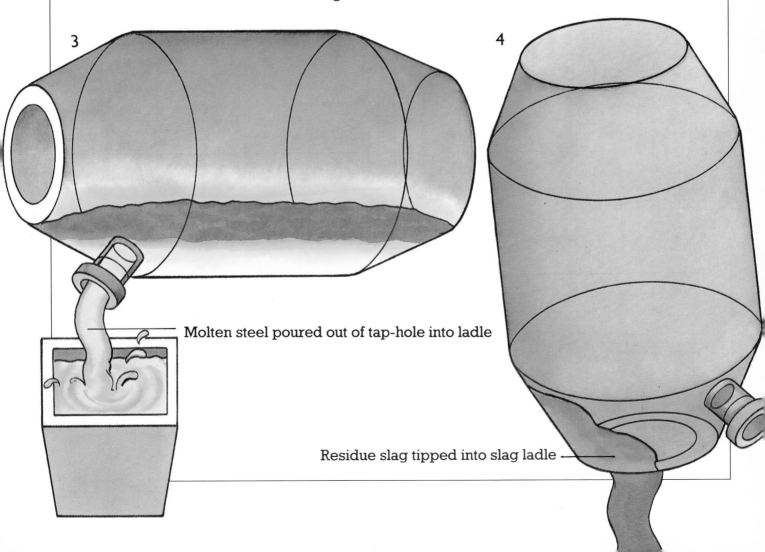

3

4

Molten steel poured out of tap-hole into ladle

Residue slag tipped into slag ladle

ALUMINUM AND COPPER

Aluminum is another very important metal. Its most useful property is that it is light and yet also can be made to be strong. It is the best cheap conductor of heat and electricity and is often used in cooking pots and electricity transmission lines. Aluminum is found combined with oxygen and other chemicals in a form called bauxite. Electricity is used to separate the metal in a process called electrolysis. The advantage of electrolysis is that it produces completely pure metal.

Electrolysis may also be used to purify metals after smelting. For example, copper is separated from its ore by smelting and then purified by electrolysis.

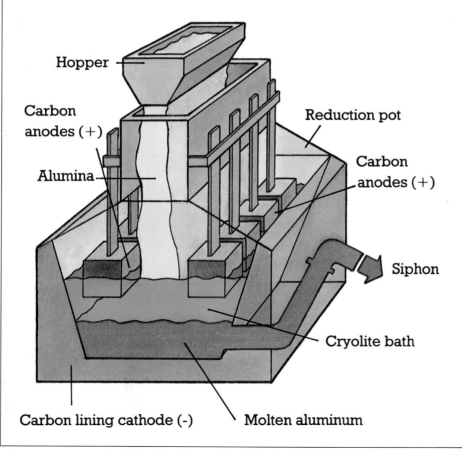

Hopper

Carbon anodes (+)

Alumina

Reduction pot

Carbon anodes (+)

Siphon

Cryolite bath

Carbon lining cathode (-)

Molten aluminum

Molten alumina (aluminum oxide) and cryolite (another aluminum compound) are poured into the reduction pot. Alumina is made up of positively charged aluminum particles and negatively charged oxygen particles. When electricity is passed through the system, the oxygen moves to the positive carbon "anodes" while the aluminum collects on the negative "cathode" floor. The pure aluminum can then be siphoned off.

Aluminum is purified through the process of electrolysis

16

Bells are often cast from bronze

COPPER AND ITS ALLOYS

Copper is one of the oldest known metals. This is because it is sometimes found naturally as lumps of pure metal. But it is also found in a range of different ores.

Copper is an excellent conductor of heat and can be used to make saucepans. It is the best low-cost conductor of electricity and can be drawn out into thin wires for electrical cables. Copper resists corrosion well and thus is used to make pipes for domestic water supplies. One of the most important properties of copper is that it blends with other metals to form a whole range of very useful alloys which are stronger than pure copper. Some of these alloys are shown below.

Brass is made by mixing copper with zinc. It is used to make machine parts as well as buttons.
Bronze is copper alloyed with tin. It can be "cast" to make statues and bells.
Copper and nickel

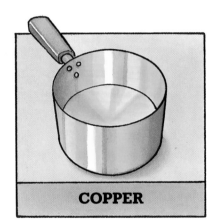

COPPER

combine to make cupronickel. Many silver-colored coins are made of this alloy. When zinc and tin are added to copper we get gunmetal which is often used in ship fittings such as anchor chains.

+ Zinc

+ Tin

+ Nickel

+ Tin and zinc

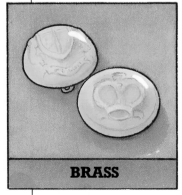

BRASS

BRONZE

CUPRONICKEL

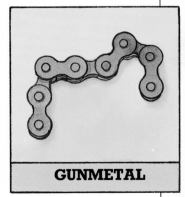

GUNMETAL

MERCURY – LIQUID METAL

Silver-colored mercury is the only metal which is a liquid at room temperature. It only becomes a solid when the temperature is lower than −39°C (−38°F). It is often nicknamed "quicksilver" because of the unusual way in which it flows.

Like other metals, mercury expands when it is heated and contracts as it cools. Mercury is particularly sensitive to changes in temperature, expanding or contracting with even small changes. These properties make mercury ideal for use in thermometers and barometers.

Most metals dissolve in mercury to form alloys known as amalgams. Dentists use gold or silver amalgams to fill holes in teeth.

Mercury is used in a thermometer because it is sensitive to heat change

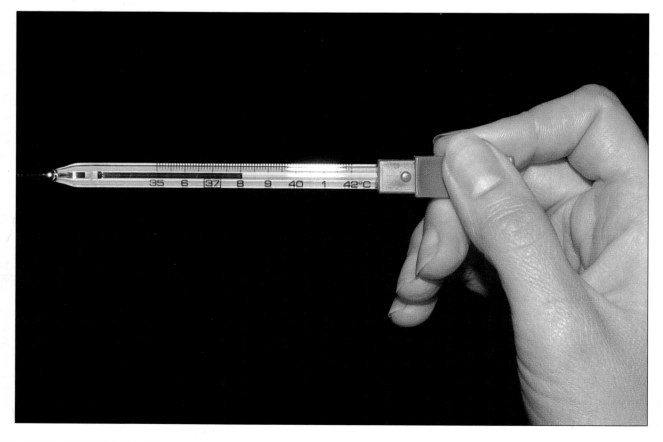

Powerful mercury vapor lamps are used to light up a football field.

PRECIOUS METALS

Gold, silver and platinum are all metals which are both rare and attractive to look at. For these reasons these metals are very highly prized and are usually used in small quantities. We most often see these metals used as decoration or as jewelry. Gold is ideal for this as it can be beaten into thin sheets or drawn out into fine wire.

But the precious metals have other more important practical uses. Gold is an excellent reflector of light and heat. It is used to coat spacecraft to protect them from the fierce heat and light of the Sun. Silver is the best conductor of electricity of all the metals and is used in circuits inside computers. Platinum is used in industry to speed up chemical reactions.

A silversmith at work

Gold is often cast into bars and stored in vaults

SHAPING METALS

Look at the metal objects around you – perhaps you can see a bicycle wheel, a key or a spoon. Each of these objects has its own special shape.

When metals are purified they are usually made into blocks or slabs. The metal then has to be shaped to make all the different objects we use. There are many different ways of shaping metal. Some metals, such as copper and gold, can be shaped while they are cold. But others, like steel, are much harder and can be more easily shaped when they are red hot. Sintering is another way of shaping metals. Metal powder is pressed into heated shapes. This technique is used for shaping magnets. The diagrams below show several other ways of shaping metals.

HOT METAL

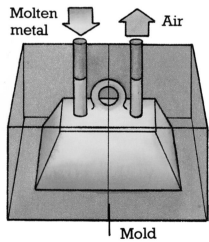

Molten metal   Air

Mold

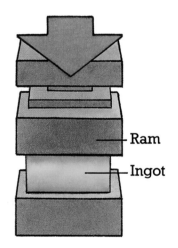

Ram

Ingot

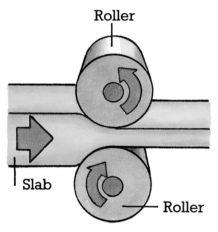

Roller

Slab

Roller

Casting
Hot liquid metal is poured into a mold where it solidifies. The mold is broken open and the metal "casting" is released.

Forging
A red hot "ingot" can be shaped by pounding with a metal "ram." Usually the bed of the forge and the ram hold two halves of a mold called a "die."

Rolling
A red hot slab may be passed backward and forward between rollers. The slab gradually gets longer and thinner – like dough under a rolling pin.

Cutting lengths of continuously cast steel

COLD METAL

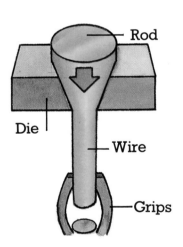
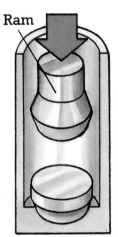
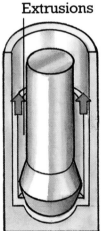
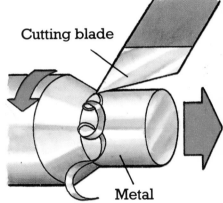

Drawing
A tempered metal rod is pulled through a die. This process is repeated through narrower dies until a long thin wire is produced.

Extrusion
Soft lead alloys can be made into thin-walled tubes by extrusion. When the ram hits the metal, the metal is forced up the sides.

Machining
Metal which has been shaped may need to be trimmed in a lathe. The rotating metal is held firmly while a sharp, hard blade trims it.

CUTTING AND JOINING

Some metal objects can be produced in one piece. But others are either so large or so complicated that they have to be built up from a number of pieces. Pieces can be cut with an oxyacetylene torch. In this torch, the gases oxygen and acetylene burn together at over 3,000°C (5,400°F) – hot enough to cut through steel by melting it. Lasers can also concentrate heat onto metal and can cut very quickly and accurately.

It is possible to join metal pieces with nuts and bolts. But nuts can work loose. They are also clumsy if the pieces to be joined are small. Welding, riveting or soldering are more permanent ways in which to join metals.

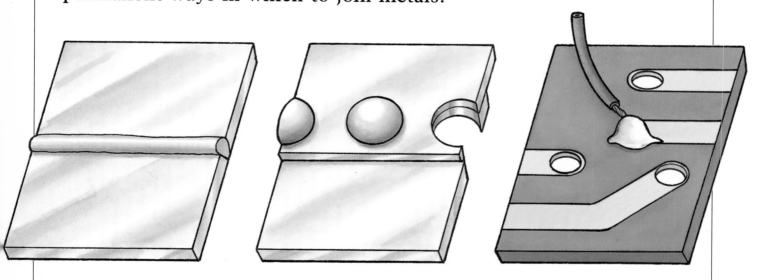

Welding
A blowtorch can be used to melt the edges of two pieces of metal. They then fuse together with some added molten metal. When the metals cool they form a strong joint.

Riveting
The rivet is pushed through holes in overlapping plates so that the pointed end pokes through. This end is hammered flat to hold the pieces tightly together.

Soldering
Soldering is used to join small pieces of metal. Solder is an alloy of tin, lead and antimony. Molten solder is applied to the joint where it fuses the pieces together.

Cutting through a sheet of metal

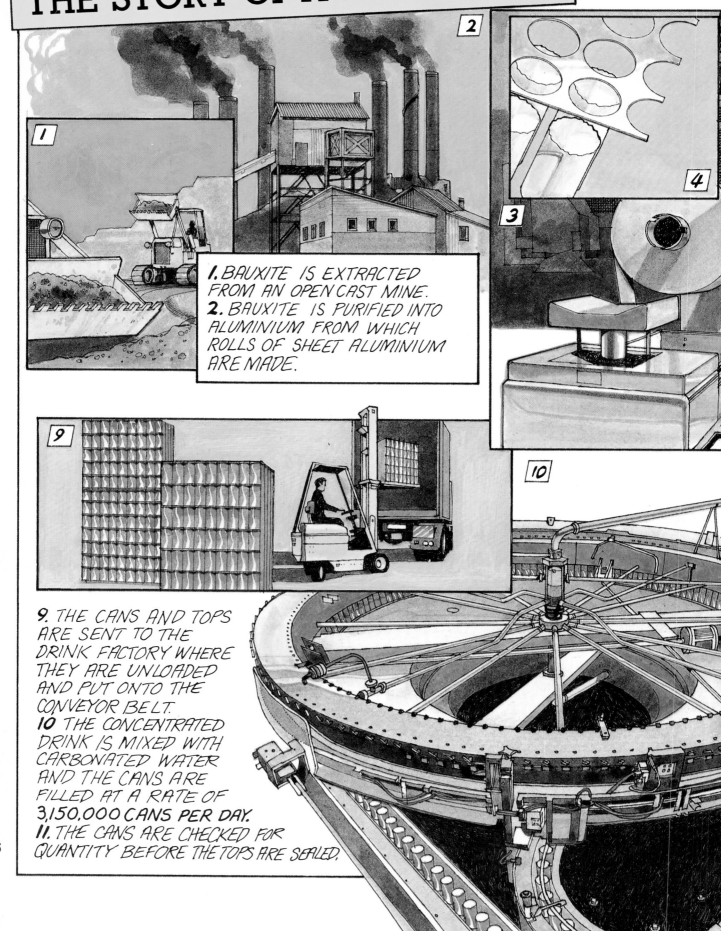

1. BAUXITE IS EXTRACTED FROM AN OPEN CAST MINE.
2. BAUXITE IS PURIFIED INTO ALUMINIUM FROM WHICH ROLLS OF SHEET ALUMINIUM ARE MADE.

9. THE CANS AND TOPS ARE SENT TO THE DRINK FACTORY WHERE THEY ARE UNLOADED AND PUT ONTO THE CONVEYOR BELT.
10 THE CONCENTRATED DRINK IS MIXED WITH CARBONATED WATER AND THE CANS ARE FILLED AT A RATE OF 3,150,000 CANS PER DAY.
11. THE CANS ARE CHECKED FOR QUANTITY BEFORE THE TOPS ARE SEALED.

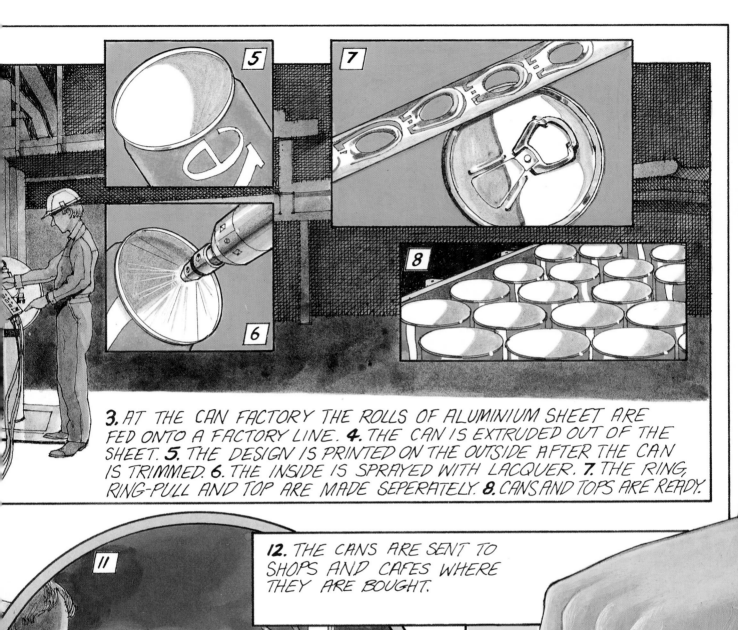

3. AT THE CAN FACTORY THE ROLLS OF ALUMINIUM SHEET ARE FED ONTO A FACTORY LINE. **4.** THE CAN IS EXTRUDED OUT OF THE SHEET. **5.** THE DESIGN IS PRINTED ON THE OUTSIDE AFTER THE CAN IS TRIMMED. **6.** THE INSIDE IS SPRAYED WITH LACQUER. **7.** THE RING, RING-PULL AND TOP ARE MADE SEPERATELY. **8.** CANS AND TOPS ARE READY.

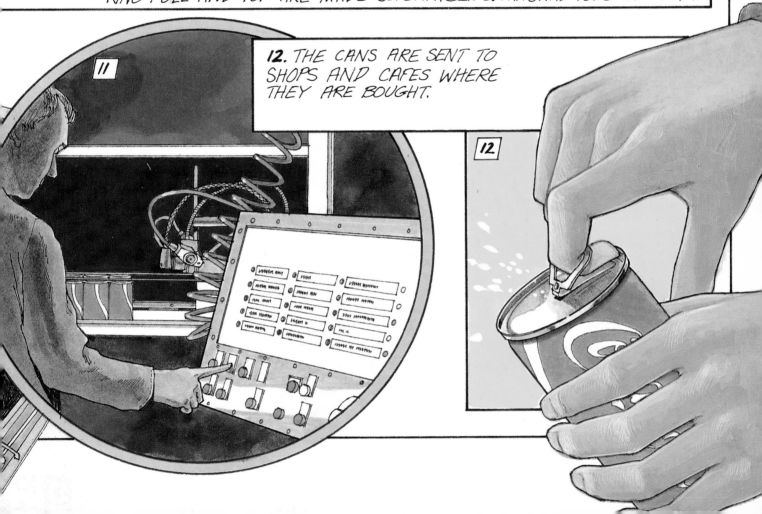

12. THE CANS ARE SENT TO SHOPS AND CAFES WHERE THEY ARE BOUGHT.

FACT FILE 1

The map below shows where some of the most important metals are mined. There are vast deposits of iron ore worldwide. The largest deposit is at Kursk, about 500 km (311 miles) south of Moscow in the USSR. It is estimated that this area has over 10 billion tons of iron ore reserves. Other large deposits are in the South Urals, North America and Australia. The two ores that contain the most iron are black magnetite and red hematite. More than 600 million tons of iron are produced each year. Pure iron is brittle, so most is made into steel by adding small amounts of carbon.

The main aluminum ore is bauxite. It is much more scarce than iron ore and is also more expensive to produce into

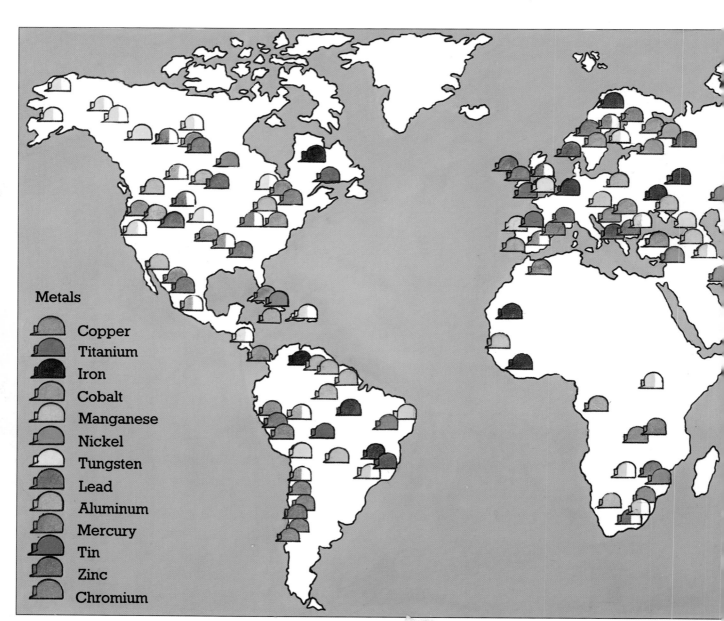

Metals

- Copper
- Titanium
- Iron
- Cobalt
- Manganese
- Nickel
- Tungsten
- Lead
- Aluminum
- Mercury
- Tin
- Zinc
- Chromium

metal. Weipa in Queensland, Australia has the world's largest bauxite deposits. Here, 25 per cent of the world's aluminum is produced, although Jamaica and Brazil and Western Australia also have huge deposits.

The copper belt of Zambia – Zaire is one of the largest copper ore deposits in the world.

Elements in the Earth's crust

Six metals – aluminum, iron, calcium, sodium, potassium and magnesium – make up just 24 per cent of the Earth's crust. Oxygen and silicon make up another 74 per cent, leaving only two per cent for all the other elements. Aluminum makes up a higher percentage than iron.

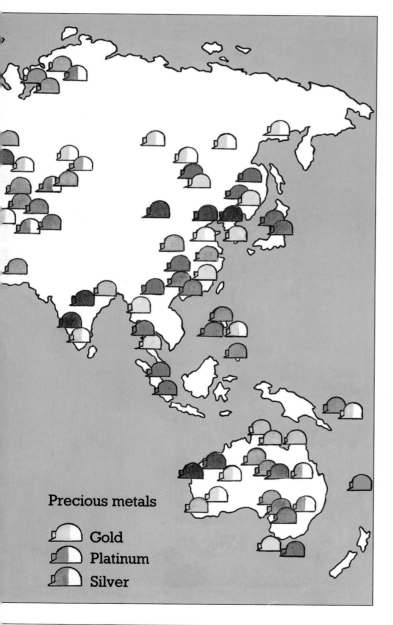

Precious metals

- Gold
- Platinum
- Silver

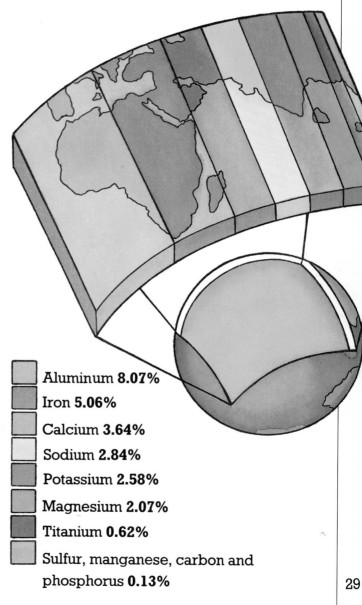

- Aluminum **8.07%**
- Iron **5.06%**
- Calcium **3.64%**
- Sodium **2.84%**
- Potassium **2.58%**
- Magnesium **2.07%**
- Titanium **0.62%**
- Sulfur, manganese, carbon and phosphorus **0.13%**

FACT FILE 2

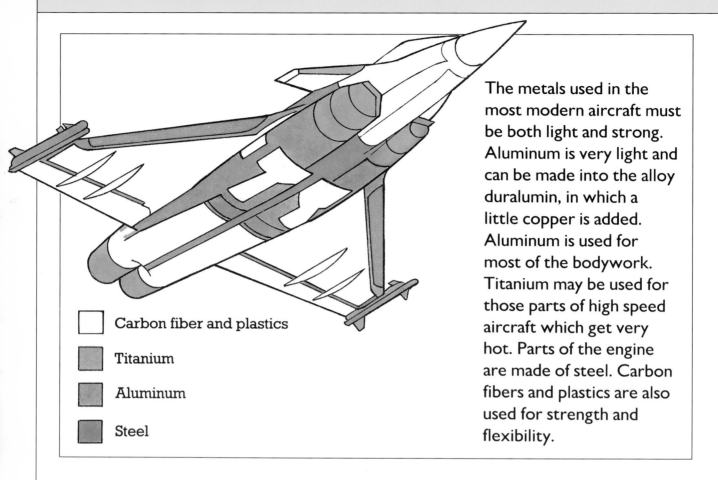

Carbon fiber and plastics

Titanium

Aluminum

Steel

The metals used in the most modern aircraft must be both light and strong. Aluminum is very light and can be made into the alloy duralumin, in which a little copper is added. Aluminum is used for most of the bodywork. Titanium may be used for those parts of high speed aircraft which get very hot. Parts of the engine are made of steel. Carbon fibers and plastics are also used for strength and flexibility.

Each metal has its own particular properties. So we may choose different metals to do different jobs. When an electric current passes through tungsten wire it glows but does not melt. This makes it ideal for lightbulbs. Forks need to be cheap and strong but must not rust. Stainless steel is a suitable choice. See if you can find out why other metals in the diagram are being used.

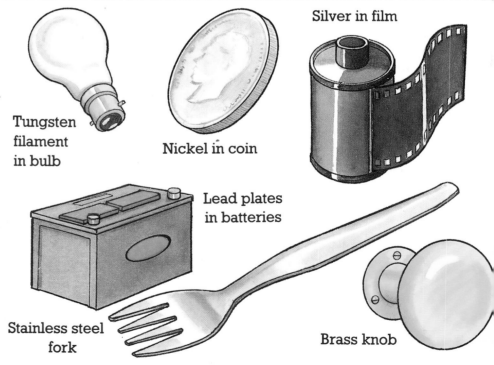

Tungsten filament in bulb

Nickel in coin

Silver in film

Lead plates in batteries

Stainless steel fork

Brass knob

Metals in a car

The ordinary car contains a huge range of metals. The bulk of the car is made of cast iron and various alloys of steel. The battery contains lead plates; all the wiring is copper; the trim is often chromium or stainless steel; and the door handles are plated zinc alloy. The wheels may be an alloy of magnesium and aluminum whereas the lightbulbs contain tungsten. The oil pump and even some engines are made of aluminum.

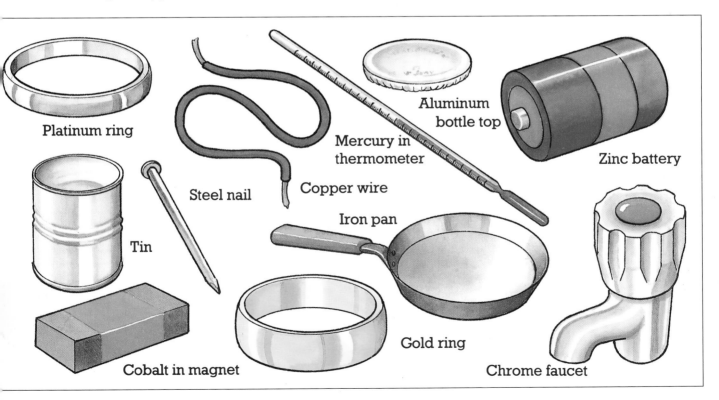

Platinum ring

Tin

Steel nail

Copper wire

Mercury in thermometer

Aluminum bottle top

Zinc battery

Iron pan

Cobalt in magnet

Gold ring

Chrome faucet

GLOSSARY

Alloy
A mixture of two or more metals which has the properties of a metal.

Anodes
Parts of an electric circuit attached to the positive terminal of the power supply.

Barometer
An instrument for measuring air pressure.

Brittle
Easily broken.

Cast
Shaped in a mold.

Cathode
Part of an electric circuit attached to the negative terminal of a power supply.

Conductor
Something which transfers heat or electricity easily from place to place.

Die
A type of mold which can be used again.

Forge
A hearth for melting and shaping metals.

Lasers
Devices which produce intense beams of light.

INDEX

PRINTED IN BELGIUM BY
proost
INTERNATIONAL BOOK PRODUCTION